Collins

Football Clubs
of
England & Scotland

Published by Collins
An imprint of HarperCollins Publishers
1 Robroyston Gate, Glasgow G33 1JN
www.collins.co.uk

HarperCollins Publishers
Macken House, 39/40 Mayor Street, Upper Dublin 1, Ireland D01 C9W8

First published 2025

© HarperCollins Publishers 2025
Text © HarperCollins Publishers 2025

Collins® is a registered trademark of HarperCollins Publishers Ltd

Commissioning Editor: Michelle I'Anson
Head of Creative Services: Craig Balfour
Art Director: Kevin Robbins
Project Leader: Robin Scrimgeour
Editorial: Richard Happer, Sheena Shanks and Andy Slater

All rights reserved. No part of this publication may be reproduced, stored in a retrieval system, or transmitted, in any form or by any means, electronic, mechanical, photocopying, recording or otherwise without the prior permission in writing of the publisher and copyright owners.

Without limiting the exclusive rights of any author, contributor or the publisher of this publication, any unauthorised use of this publication to train generative artificial intelligence (AI) technologies is expressly prohibited. HarperCollins also exercise their rights under Article 4(3) of the Digital Single Market Directive 2019/790 and expressly reserve this publication from the text and data mining exception.

The contents of this publication are believed correct at the time of printing. Nevertheless the publisher can accept no responsibility for errors or omissions, changes in the detail given or for any expense or loss thereby caused.

A catalogue record for this book is available from the British Library.

ISBN 978-0-00-875182-1

10 9 8 7 6 5 4 3 2 1

Printed in India

MIX
Paper | Supporting
responsible forestry
FSC™ C007454

Collins

Football Clubs

of
England & Scotland

FUN FOOTBALL FACTS, STATS & QUIZZES

Contents

▷▷▷ Introduction 6

How to use this book 7

Football Clubs of England   8

Football Clubs of Scotland   114

Facts & Stats 163

Quizzes 177

Introduction

Are you ready to find out about all the football clubs of England and Scotland?

Clubs play in many different colours, and some kits have designs like stripes or hoops.

Discover where each club plays, how old they are, who is their all-time top scorer, and find out a fascinating fact!

Clubs are listed alphabetically within each country, to help you find the one you are looking for.

Every club has its fans... which is your favourite?

How to use this book

The English football league is divided into four divisions (tiers):

Premier League

Championship

League One

League Two

Clubs are promoted (go up) and relegated (go down) between these divisions each season.

Below this is the National League.

Clubs are promoted and relegated between the National League and League Two each season.

Some Welsh clubs play in the league. Some clubs that used to be in the English football league are included in the 'Other English clubs' section, starting on page 102.

Football Clubs of England

Accrington Stanley
(Stanley)

1968   Crown Ground   5,450   Billy Kee 83

The original Accrington Stanley were formed in 1891 and played in the Football League for 41 years. The current club has been in the league since 2006.

Arsenal

(The Gunners)

1886　　Emirates Stadium　　60,704　　Thierry Henry 228

Arsenal set a national record of 49 games unbeaten between May 2003 and October 2004. They won the Premier League in 2003/04 without losing a match.

Aston Villa
(The Villans)

1874   Villa Park   42,785   Billy Walker 244

The Birmingham club scored 128 goals in season 1930/31, which is still a record for England's top league division.

Barnet

(The Bees)

1888 • The Hive Stadium • 6,500 • Arthur Morris 403

In 1947, Barnet won 5-3 in a friendly against Sing Tao Sports Club, the first Chinese team to ever play in Britain. Barnet have been in and out of the Football League since 1991.

Barnsley

(The Reds)

1887   Oakwell   23,287   Ernie Hine 131

Barnsley have played more games in the second-top division of English football than any other team. They weren't promoted or relegated at all between 1898 and 1932.

Barrow

(The Bluebirds)

1901　　Holker Street　　6,500　　Colin Cowperthwaite 282

Barrow's club badge features a submarine. They have been built in the team's home town of Barrow-in-Furness since the club was formed.

Birmingham City
(Blues)

1875　　St Andrew's　　29,409　　Joe Bradford 267

Birmingham were the first English team to play in a major European final. They lost to Barcelona in the final of the Inter-Cities Fairs Cup in 1960.

Blackburn Rovers
(Rovers)

1875   Ewood Park   31,367   Simon Garner 194

Blackburn Rovers are the only surviving club to have won the FA Cup three times in a row – in 1884, 1885 and 1886.

Blackpool
(The Seasiders)

 1887

 Bloomfield Road

 16,616

 Jimmy Hampson 252

Blackpool are European trophy winners – they won the 1971 Anglo-Italian Cup, beating Bologna 2-1 in the final.

Bolton Wanderers
(The Trotters)

1874   Toughsheet Community Stadium   28,723   Nat Lofthouse 285

Bolton have played 73 seasons in England's top division – the most of any club that has not won the title.

AFC Bournemouth
(The Cherries)

 1899

 Vitality Stadium

 11,329

 Ron Eyre 229

Originally called Boscombe (the part of Bournemouth they come from), the club became Bournemouth & Boscombe Athletic in 1923. They have had their current name since 1971.

Bradford City
(The Bantams)

 1903

 Valley Parade

 24,840

 James Hanson 334

Bradford are the only professional club in England to have the colours claret and amber on their strip.

Brentford

(The Bees)

1889   Gtech Community Stadium   17,250   Jim Towers 163

In season 1929/30, the London team set a record by winning all of their 21 home league matches, in the Third Division South.

Brighton & Hove Albion
(The Seagulls)

1901   American Express Community Stadium   31,876   Tommy Cook 123

From 1920 until 2011, when Crawley Town were promoted, Brighton were the only team from Sussex in the English football league.

Bristol City

(The Robins)

1894   Ashton Gate Stadium   27,000   John Atyeo 351

The Robins have had several other nicknames over the years, including the Garibaldians, Reds, Red Shirts, Citizens, Cidereds and the Bristol Babe.

Bristol Rovers

(The Pirates)

1883   Memorial Stadium   12,534   Geoff Bradford 242

Bristol Rovers are one of only two clubs that play in tops with a quarters design (Wycombe Wanderers is the other).

Bromley

(The Ravens)

1892   Hayes Lane   5,300   George Brown 570

The biggest-ever crowd at a Bromley game was 10,798 in 1948. They lost 3-1 in a friendly with the national team of Nigeria, who played barefoot.

Burnley
(The Clarets)

1882　　　Turf Moor　　　21,944　　　George Beel 188

Burnley player William Tait was the first player in English league history to score a hat-trick. He did so in a 4-3 win over Bolton, on the second day of the first season in 1888.

Burton Albion

(Brewers)

1950   Pirelli Stadium   6,912   Richie Barker 159

The club from Burton upon Trent joined the league in 2009.
They have played as high as the Championship, having been promoted two years in a row, in 2015 and 2016.

Cambridge United
(The U's)

1912 | Abbey Stadium | 8,127 | Russell Crane 186

In the 1920s, when the club was called Abbey United, their ground was known as the 'Celery Trenches' due to its poor pitch. The away dressing room was at a nearby pub.

Cardiff City

(The Bluebirds)

1899

Cardiff City Stadium

33,280

Len Davies 179

Cardiff are the only non-English club to have won the FA Cup. They lifted the trophy in 1927, beating Arsenal 1-0 in the final.

Charlton Athletic
(The Addicks)

 1905

 The Valley

 27,111

 Derek Hales 168

Charlton got their unusual nickname from the haddock ('addick' in the local accent) and chips served after the game by a nearby fishmonger.

Chelsea

(The Blues)

1905 Stamford Bridge 41,631 Frank Lampard 211

Chelsea are the only club to have won all three major European competitions twice – the Champions League, Europa League and Cup Winners' Cup.

Cheltenham Town
(The Robins)

 1887

 Whaddon Road

 7,066

 Dave Lewis 290

In the 2023/24 season, Cheltenham didn't score a single goal in their opening 11 matches, equalling a Football League record.

Chesterfield
(The Spireites)

1919   SMH Group Stadium   10,504   Ernie Moss 162

An earlier version of the club was called Chesterfield Town. In the 1890s, they wore a Union Jack on their shirt. This kit had been left behind by another old Chesterfield team, Spital.

Colchester United
(The U's)

1937

Colchester Community Stadium

10,105

Tony Adcock 149

Colchester's badge uniquely features a Roman eagle. The city is the oldest in Britain and was a Roman garrison.

Coventry City
(The Sky Blues)

1883

Coventry Building Society Arena

32,609

Clarrie Bourton 182

Coventry were the first club in England to have an all-seater stadium, when their old Highfield Road ground was converted in 1981.

Crawley Town
(The Red Devils)

1896 **Broadfield Stadium** **5,996** **Matt Tubbs 66**

Crawley earned promotion to the Football League in 2011 by winning the Conference division with a record-breaking total of 105 points.

Crewe Alexandra
(The Railwaymen)

1877　　Gresty Road　　10,153　　Bert Swindells 128

Crewe are named after Princess Alexandra of Denmark, the wife of King Edward VII, who was the Princess of Wales when the club was founded in 1877.

Crystal Palace

(The Eagles)

1905　　Selhurst Park　　25,456　　Peter Simpson 165

Palace's 2025 FA Cup final win, beating Manchester City, was the first in their history. They had lost to Manchester United in both of their other two final appearances.

Derby County
(The Rams)

 1884

 Pride Park Stadium

 32,956

 Steve Bloomer 332

In 2008, Derby set some unwanted records – they scored the fewest points ever in a season with just 11, and went 36 consecutive league games without a win.

Doncaster Rovers
(Rovers)

1879 — Eco-Power Stadium — 15,231 — Tom Keetley 186

The club's first shirts were navy blue with a yellow diagonal cross. At that time, players also wore a blue tam-o'-shanter cap!

Everton

(The Toffees)

1878　　Hill Dickinson Stadium　　52,888　　Dixie Dean 363

Everton have played more seasons in the top division of the English league than any other club – 122 by season 2024/25.

Exeter City

(The Grecians)

1901   St James Park   8,720   Tony Kellow 129

The great footballing nation of Brazil played its first-ever game against... Exeter City! The club was on tour in South America in 1914 when the game was set up. Exeter lost 2-0.

Fleetwood Town
(The Fishermen)

1908

Highbury Stadium

5,327

Dave Barnes 101

Fleetwood won their sixth promotion in ten years when they beat Burton Albion at Wembley in the League Two play-off final in 2014.

Fulham

(The Cottagers)

 1879

 Craven Cottage

 29,600

 Gordon Davies 178

Fulham are the oldest professional football club in London.
Their famous fans include actor Hugh Grant, actress Margot Robbie and presenter/novelist Richard Osman.

Gillingham
(The Gills)

1893 — Priestfield Stadium — 11,582 — Brian Yeo 149

Despite being founded in 1893, Gillingham didn't win their first trophy until 2000. The Gills won the Second Division play-off final with a 3-2 victory over Wigan Athletic.

Grimsby Town
(The Mariners)

1878　　Blundell Park　　9,052　　Pat Glover 180

In 2022/23, Grimsby Town became the first team in FA Cup history to beat five teams from higher league divisions.

Harrogate Town

(Sulphurites)

 1919

 Wetherby Road

 5,000

 Jim Hague 135

Harrogate's home match against Port Vale on 5 April 2021 was the first English football league game to be refereed by a woman, Rebecca Welch.

Huddersfield Town
(The Terriers)

1908 — Kirklees Stadium — 24,121 — George Brown 159

Huddersfield Town were the first English team to win three league titles in a row. They were crowned champions in 1924, 1925 and 1926.

Hull City

(The Tigers)

1903

MKM Stadium

25,586

Chris Chilton 222

In 1970, Hull became the first team in the world to be knocked out of a cup competition in a penalty shoot-out. Manchester United beat them in a Watney Cup semi-final.

Ipswich Town
(Tractor Boys)

1878

Portman Road

29,673

Ray Crawford 218

Ipswich are undefeated at home in all European competitions, a record that stretches back to 1962. They've beaten Real Madrid, AC Milan, Inter Milan, Lazio and Barcelona at Portman Road.

Leeds United

(The Whites)

1919   Elland Road   37,608   Peter Lorimer 238

In 1968, Leeds became the first English team to win the Inter-Cities Fairs Cup. This trophy later became the UEFA Cup, and then the Europa League.

Leicester City

(The Foxes)

1884   King Power Stadium   32,262   Arthur Chandler 273

Leicester's Jamie Vardy set a record when he scored in 11 consecutive matches during Leicester's 2015/16 Premier League-winning season.

Leyton Orient
(The O's)

1881   Brisbane Road   9,271   Tommy Johnston 121

At full-time in an FA Cup match in 2010, Orient were drawing with Droylsden 2-2. Then the O's scored a record 6 goals in extra time to win 8-2.

Lincoln City
(The Imps)

 1884

 Sincil Bank

 10,669

 Andy Graver 143

In 1976, Lincoln won the bottom division with the highest number of points (74) then awarded in any division. At that time, a win was worth 2 points.

Liverpool
(The Reds)

1892　　Anfield　　61,276　　Ian Rush 346

Liverpool have won the European Cup/Champions League 6 times. This is 3 times more than any other British club.

Luton Town
(The Hatters)

 1885

 Kenilworth Road

 12,000

 Gordon Turner 276

Between 2007 and 2009, Luton were relegated three seasons in a row, dropping out of the league. However, by 2023, they had climbed all the way back up to the Premier League.

Manchester City

(The Citizens)

1880 | Etihad Stadium | 55,097 | Sergio Agüero 260

Manchester City hosted the largest crowd for an English club football game on 3 March 1934 – 84,569 watched them beat Stoke City 1-0 in the FA Cup at Maine Road. This record still stands.

Manchester United
(The Red Devils)

 1878

 Old Trafford

 74,879

 Wayne Rooney 253

In 1999, Manchester United became the first English team to win the treble of the Premier League, FA Cup and UEFA Champions League.

Mansfield Town
(The Stags)

1897　　Field Mill　　9,186　　Harry Johnson 114

Mansfield's ground, Field Mill, was first used in 1861, making it the oldest ground used purely for football in the Football League.

Middlesbrough
(Boro)

1876   Riverside Stadium   34,742   George Camsell 345

Middlesbrough were the first football club in the world to launch their own TV channel. Boro TV was launched in 1997, one year ahead of Manchester United's MUTV.

Millwall

(The Lions)

1885   The Den   20,146   Neil Harris 138

Founded by workers on the Isle of Dogs in London, the club have been known as Millwall Rovers, Millwall Athletic, and now simply 'Millwall'.

Milton Keynes Dons
(The Dons)

2004

Stadium MK

30,500

Izale McLeod 71

MK Dons were born when Wimbledon FC decided to move out of London. For their first three seasons, they played their home games at the National Hockey Stadium.

Newcastle United
(The Magpies)

 1881

 St James' Park

 52,405

 Alan Shearer 206

Newcastle's original kit was red shirts and white shorts – the famous black and white stripes were not used until 1894.

Newport County

(The Exiles)

1912 — Rodney Parade — 7,850 — Reg Parker 99

Newport were originally nicknamed 'The Ironsides' after the nearby steelworks. But when they were evicted from their ground, they called themselves 'The Exiles'.

Northampton Town
(The Cobblers)

1897

Sixfields Stadium

7,798

Jack English 143

The Cobblers hold the record for the shortest time taken to be promoted from the lowest league division to the top division, then relegated back to the lowest division, between 1960 and 1969.

Norwich City

(The Canaries)

1902 | Carrow Road | 27,359 | Johnny Gavin 122

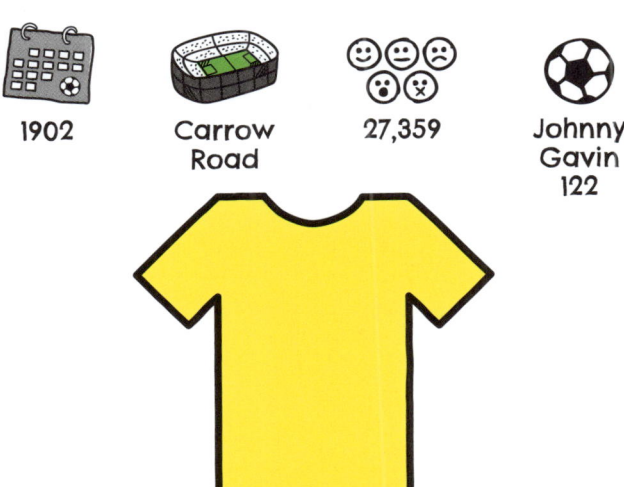

Norwich City fans sing a song called 'On The Ball, City'. Written in the 1890s, it is the world's oldest football chant.

Nottingham Forest
(Forest)

1865   City Ground   30,445   Grenville Morris 217

Nottingham Forest were the last British club to win the European Cup twice in a row. They triumphed in 1979 and 1980.

Notts County

(The Magpies)

1862   Meadow Lane   19,841   Les Bradd 137

Formed in 1862, Notts County are the oldest professional football club in the world. They were relegated from the top division in 1992, so missed out on the first Premier League season.

Oldham Athletic

(Latics)

1895　　Boundary Park　　13,560　　Roger Palmer 141

Latics (short for Athletic) were one of the founding members of the top-flight Premier League when it was formed in 1992. They came back up from the National League in 2025.

Oxford United

(The U's)

1893 Kassam Stadium 12,500 Graham Atkinson 107

Oxford United wasn't the club's name until 1960. They were formed in 1893 by a doctor and a vicar, and initially named after the local town, Headington.

Peterborough United
(The Posh)

1934   London Road Stadium   13,511   Jim Hall 122

The manager of a previous Peterborough club once said he was looking for "posh (good) players for a posh team." This gave them their nickname, which is still used today.

Plymouth Argyle

(The Pilgrims)

1886

Home Park

17,900

Sammy Black 184

Plymouth Argyle get their nickname from the Pilgrim Fathers, who sailed from Plymouth on the 'Mayflower'. They are the most southerly and westerly league club in England.

Port Vale

(The Valiants)

1876   Vale Park   15,036   Wilf Kirkham 164

Port Vale hold the record for the most seasons in the English football league without reaching the top tier – 113 by the end of the 2024/25 season.

Portsmouth
(Pompey)

1898   Fratton Park   20,899   Peter Harris 194

Portsmouth are the only professional club in England not located on mainland Great Britain. Their Fratton Park ground lies on Portsea Island.

Preston North End
(The Lilywhites)

1880 — Deepdale — 23,404 — Tom Finney 210

In 1889, Preston became the first team to win 'the Double' – the league championship and the FA Cup.

Queens Park Rangers
(The R's)

 1882

 Loftus Road

 18,439

 George Goddard 186

QPR hold the league record for the number of home grounds. They played in at least 12 different stadiums before finding a long-term home at Loftus Road in 1917.

Reading
(The Royals)

1871　　Madejski Stadium　　24,161　　Trevor Senior 191

In 2010, Reading's Jimmy Kébé scored the fastest goal ever in the FA Cup. He netted after just 9 seconds in a 5th round tie against West Bromwich Albion.

Rotherham United
(The Millers)

1925 — New York Stadium — 12,021 — Gladstone Guest 130

Rotherham lost the first League Cup final to Aston Villa in 1961. They won the first leg 2-0 but lost the second leg 3-0, after extra time.

Salford City
(The Ammies)

1940   Moor Lane   5,108   Matt Smith 44

Salford is part-owned by former Manchester United 'Class of 92' players David Beckham and Gary Neville. Nicky Butt, Ryan Giggs, Phil Neville and Paul Scholes are also involved.

Sheffield United
(The Blades)

1889   Bramall Lane   32,050   Harry Johnson 201

Built in 1855, Bramall Lane is the oldest football league ground in the world. The first game there was played in 1862, when Sheffield FC and Hallam drew 0-0.

Sheffield Wednesday
(The Owls)

 1867

 Hillsborough Stadium

 39,732

 Johnny Fantham 141

The fastest shot recorded in the Premier League was by Sheffield Wednesday's David Hirst in 1996 against Arsenal. He hit the bar with a shot recorded at 114 mph (183 km/h).

Shrewsbury Town
(The Shrews)

1886 — New Meadow — 9,875 — Arthur Rowle 152

Former England goalkeeper Joe Hart began his career with Shrewsbury in 2003. He is one of only two men to win every major domestic trophy in both England and Scotland.

Southampton
(The Saints)

1885

St Mary's Stadium

32,384

Mick Channon 228

The fastest Premier League hat-trick was scored by Southampton's Sadio Mané. In 2015, he scored three times in 2 minutes 56 seconds against Aston Villa.

Stevenage

(The Boro)

1976　　Broadhall Way　　7,800　　Martin Gittings 217

Stevenage only started playing senior football in 1980 but enjoyed instant success. They won the United Counties Division One and League Cup double in their first year.

Stockport County
(The Hatters)

1883   Edgeley Park   10,852   Jack Connor 140

Stockport used to play their home games on a Friday night so they wouldn't clash with their neighbours Manchester United and Manchester City.

Stoke City
(The Potters)

1863   **bet365 Stadium**   **30,089**   **John Ritchie 176**

Stoke City are the world's second-oldest professional football club after Notts County. They are the oldest team to have played in the Premier League.

Sunderland
(The Black Cats)

1879   Stadium of Light   49,000   Bobby Gurney 228

In 1893, Sunderland were the first team to score 100 goals in a season. It took 27 years for another team to match this.

Swansea City

(The Swans)

1912　　Swansea.com　　21,088　　Ivor
　　　　Stadium　　　　　　　　　Allchurch
　　　　　　　　　　　　　　　　166

In 2013, Swansea became the first Welsh club to win the League Cup, beating Bradford City 5-0. This was also the highest-ever winning margin in the final.

Swindon Town

(The Robins)

1879 — County Ground — 15,728 — Harry Morris 229

John Trollope set an English record for most league appearances by a player at one club. He played in 770 league games for Swindon between 1960 and 1981. His record stood for 43 years.

Tottenham Hotspur
(Spurs)

 1882

 Tottenham Hotspur Stadium

 62,850

 Harry Kane 280

Spurs became the first British club to win a European trophy when they lifted the European Cup Winners' Cup in 1963.

Tranmere Rovers
(The Rovers)

1884   Prenton Park   16,789   Ian Muir 180

Harold Bell did not miss a single match for Tranmere Rovers for 9 years. He played in 401 consecutive games between 1946 and 1955.

Walsall
(The Saddlers)

 1888

 Bescot Stadium

 11,300

 Alan Buckley 202

The current club was formed when two separate clubs, Walsall Town and Walsall Swifts, joined together. They were originally called Walsall Town Swifts.

Watford

(The Hornets)

 1881

 Vicarage Road

 22,200

 Luther Blissett 186

Pop star Elton John was the chairman of Watford from 1976-1990 and 1994-2002. He saw the club climb from the bottom division to finishing 2nd in the top division in just 6 years.

West Bromwich Albion
(The Baggies)

1878   The Hawthorns   26,850   Tony Brown 279

West Bromwich Albion hold the record for the biggest victory in England's top league division. They beat Darwen 12-0 in April 1892.

West Ham United
(The Hammers)

 1895

 London Stadium

 62,500

 Vic Watson 326

Three West Ham players were in England's World Cup-winning team of 1966 – Martin Peters, the captain Bobby Moore and Geoff Hurst, who scored a famous hat-trick.

Wigan Athletic
(Latics)

 1932

 Brick Community Stadium

 25,138

 Andy Liddell 70

Wigan beat Carlisle United 6-1 in the 1935/36 FA Cup - a record victory for a non-league club against league opposition.

AFC Wimbledon
(The Dons)

 2002

 Plough Lane

 9,369

 Kevin Cooper 104

This new club was formed after Wimbledon FC moved to Milton Keynes to become MK Dons. They were promoted from the 9th tier to the 3rd tier in the space of 13 years.

Wolverhampton Wanderers
(Wolves)

 1877

 Molineux

 31,700

 Steve Bull 306

Wolves were the first team to win all four divisions of the English football league when they won the third tier title in 1988/89.

Wrexham
(The Red Dragons)

 1864

 Racecourse Ground

 13,341

 Tommy Bamford 175

Wrexham are the oldest professional club in Wales and the third-oldest in the world. They are currently owned by Hollywood stars Ryan Reynolds and Rob McElhenney.

Wycombe Wanderers
(The Chairboys)

 1887

 Adams Park

 10,137

 Tony Horseman 416

Wycombe's mascot is called Bodger, after the club's record goal-scorer, Tony 'Bodger' Horseman. Their home town of High Wycombe is famous for chair-making.

Other English clubs

Aldershot

The Shots usually play in a red and blue kit, reflecting their close links to the British Army. Original club Aldershot FC were reformed in 1992 as Aldershot Town.

Boston United

Despite being an east coast club, the Pilgrims once played in the West Midlands League. They spent 5 seasons in the bottom division of the senior league, from 2002 until 2007.

Bury

In the early 1900s, the Shakers were an established top-flight side and won the FA Cup twice. They were expelled from the Football League in 2019.

Carlisle United

Carlisle's badge features two red wyverns – mythical dragons that are also on the city's coat of arms. The Cumbrians were relegated to the National League in 2025.

Chester

Original club Chester City went bust in 2010 but were soon reborn as Chester FC. The Seals' biggest local rivals are in a different country – Wrexham in Wales.

Dagenham & Redbridge

Formed in 1992, Dagenham & Redbridge are also known as the Daggers. They played in the Football League from 2007 to 2016, including one season in the third tier.

Darlington

The Quakers' badge features a steam train – the world's first passenger railway ran to Darlington in 1825. The club were relegated from the Football League in 2010.

Forest Green Rovers

FGR became the world's first vegan football club in 2015 and were certified carbon neutral in 2018. They returned to the National League in 2024, after back-to-back relegations.

Halifax Town

The Shaymen dropped out of the Football League in 2002. Future Leicester and England star Jamie Vardy helped the club win promotion to the Conference North league in 2011.

Hartlepool United

H'Angus the Monkey, the club's mascot, was elected mayor of Hartlepool in 2002. His campaign slogan was 'Free bananas for schoolchildren'.

Hereford United

Graham Turner managed Hereford United for 14 seasons, one of the longest spells in English football. After the Bulls went bust in 2014, a new club was formed – Hereford FC.

Kidderminster Harriers

Harriers have played at the same home ground, Aggborough Stadium, since 1890. They played in the bottom division of the Football League between 2000 and 2005.

Macclesfield Town

The team were nicknamed 'The Silkmen' as Macclesfield was once home to lots of silk-making factories. After going bust in 2020, they were reborn as Macclesfield FC.

Maidstone United

The Stones only played in the Football League for 3 years, before going bust in 1992. They reformed as Maidstone Invicta, later changing back to the original club's name.

Morecambe

When the Shrimps won promotion from the Conference league in 2007, the crowd of 40,043 was the largest in a league play-off final at the time.

Rochdale

The Dale have played at Spotland Stadium since they joined the Football League in 1921. After 102 years, the club were relegated to the National League in 2023.

Rushden & Diamonds

The Diamonds played in the Football League from 2001 to 2006. They went bust in 2011 and were succeeded by new club AFC Rushden & Diamonds.

Scarborough

In 1987, the Seadogs became the first team to win automatic promotion from the Conference to the Football League. They folded in 2007 and new club Scarborough Athletic was formed.

Scunthorpe United

When it opened in 1988, Scunthorpe's Glanford Park was the first new Football League stadium built in England for 33 years. 'The Iron' were relegated to the National League in 2022.

Southend United

Southend United are known as the Shrimpers, thanks to the town's maritime history. After 101 years in the Football League, they were relegated in 2021.

Sutton United

One of Sutton's nicknames is 'The Amber and Chocolates' as their kit used to include brown stripes. The club competed in the Scottish Challenge Cup in 2018.

Torquay United

Relegated from the Football League in 2023, the Gulls play in a yellow strip with blue shorts that reflects the sand and sea colours of their coastal home.

Yeovil Town

After playing as high as the Championship, the Glovers lost league status in 2019. Their old home pitch at Huish was famous for its 2.4 metre (8 ft) slope from corner to corner.

York City

York's ground was once known as KitKat Crescent thanks to sponsorship from Nestlé. Nicknamed 'The Minstermen' (after York Minster cathedral), they dropped into the National League in 2016.

The Scottish football league is divided into four divisions (tiers):

Premiership

Championship

League One

League Two

Clubs are promoted and relegated between these divisions each season.

Below this are the Highland League and the Lowland League.

The champions of these face each other in the pyramid play-off. The winner then competes with the club finishing bottom of League Two for a place in the league.

Some clubs that used to be in the Scottish football league are included in the 'Other Scottish clubs' section, starting on page 158.

Football Clubs of Scotland

Aberdeen

(The Dons)

1903 | Pittodrie Stadium | 20,866 | Joe Harper 199

Aberdeen are the only Scottish team to have won two European trophies. They lifted both the Cup Winners' Cup and the European Super Cup in 1983.

Airdrieonians
(Airdrie, The Diamonds)

2002   Excelsior Stadium   10,101   Calum Gallacher 69

Formed in 2002 after the original club of this name went bankrupt. They were initially called Airdrie United, but changed to Airdrieonians in 2013.

Alloa Athletic

(The Wasps)

1878

Recreation Park

3,100

Willie Irvine 91

It's no surprise where Alloa got their nickname from. For over 100 years, the Wasps have worn a strip with gold and black stripes.

Annan Athletic

(The Galabankies)

 1942
 Galabank
 2,504
 Aidan Smith 84

Between 1952 and 1977, Annan Athletic played in the Carlisle and District League in England. They joined the Scottish Football League in 2008.

Arbroath

(The Red Lichties)

1878

Gayfield Park

6,600

Bobby Linn 85

Arbroath hold the world record for the biggest victory in senior football. On 12 September 1885 they beat Bon Accord 36-0 in a Scottish Cup match.

Ayr United
(The Honest Men)

1910 | Somerset Park | 10,185 | Peter Price 213

Ayr's nickname of 'The Honest Men' comes from the famous Robert Burns poem 'Tam o' Shanter'. Burns was born in Ayrshire.

Celtic

(The Bhoys)

1887   Celtic Park   60,411   Jimmy McGrory 522

In 1967, Celtic became the first British team to win the European Cup. Amazingly, the match squad was made up of players all born within 30 miles of Glasgow.

Clyde
(The Bully Wee)

1877   New Douglas Park   6,018   Tommy Ring 124

After leaving Rutherglen in 1986, Clyde ground-shared with Partick Thistle and Hamilton Accies. They then spent 28 years in Cumbernauld but now once more play in Hamilton.

Cove Rangers
(The Toonsers)

1922   Balmoral Stadium   3,023   Mike Beattie 318

Before they joined the senior leagues, the Aberdeen-based club won the treble in 2001 – Highland League, Aberdeenshire Shield and Scottish Qualifying Cup.

Dumbarton

(The Sons)

1872 | Dumbarton Football Stadium | 2,020 | Hugh Gallacher 205

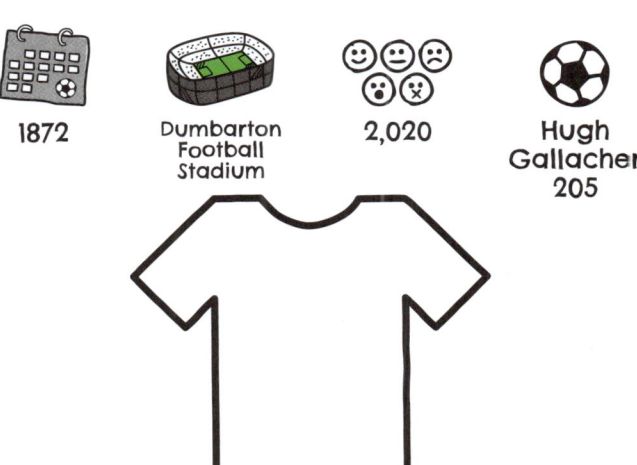

The club's unusual nickname comes from 'Sons of the Rock' – Dumbarton is famous for its landmark rock with a castle on top. The stadium is in its shadow.

Dundee

(The Dee, The Dark Blues)

1893 — Dens Park — 11,775 — Andy Gilzean 113

Dens Park is only 200 yards (183 metres) away from Tannadice, the home of Dundee's city rivals United. In 1925, the first derby between the teams, ended 0-0.

Dundee United
(The Tangerines, The Terrors)

1909   Tannadice Park   14,223   Peter McKay 202

Dundee United are the only British team to have a 100% record against Barcelona in European fixtures – 4 wins out of 4 matches.

Dunfermline Athletic
(The Pars)

 1885

 East End Park

 11,480

 Charlie Dickson 212

Two former Dunfermline players have gone on to manage Manchester United – Sir Alex Ferguson and David Moyes.

East Fife

(The Fifers)

 1903

 Bayview Stadium

 1,980

 Phil Weir 228

In 1938, East Fife made history when they became the first club from outside the top league to win the Scottish Cup. They beat Kilmarnock in the final, after a replay.

East Kilbride
(The Kilby)

 2010

 K-Park Training Academy

 700

 Cameron Elliott 46

The original East Kilbride FC were formed in 1871, but didn't last long. In 2025, the new club joined the Scottish Football League, winning the play-off at their fourth attempt.

Edinburgh City

(The Citizens)

1966　　　Meadowbank Stadium　　　1,280　　　Blair Henderson 53

Edinburgh City started out as Postal United FC – an amateur team made up of postal workers. They were the first club to join the league through the pyramid play-off.

Elgin City

(City)

 1893

 Borough Briggs

 4,520

 Gerry Graham 371

Elgin's home pitch at Borough Briggs is the most northerly football league ground in the United Kingdom. The club joined the Scottish Football League in 2000.

Falkirk

(The Bairns)

1876 — Falkirk Stadium — 7,937 — Kenneth Dawson 237

In 1922, Falkirk signed striker Syd Puddefoot from West Ham United. The transfer fee of £5,000 broke the world record at the time.

Forfar Athletic
(The Loons)

1885   Station Park   6,777   John Clark 127

A 'loon' in the north-east of Scotland is another word for a young man. The club is also known as the 'Sky Blues' – one of the team's colours.

Greenock Morton

(Morton, The Ton)

1874

Cappielow Park

11,589

Allan McGraw 117

From 1993 to 1995, Morton wore tartan kits (blue for home and red for away). The blue version was revived as an away kit in 2005.

Hamilton Academical
(The Accies)

1874 — Broadwood Stadium — 8,086 — David Wilson 246

The Accies are the only professional club in British football to be formed from a school team. The team was started by the pupils and rector of Hamilton Academy.

Heart of Midlothian
(Hearts, The Jam Tarts)

1874

Tynecastle Park

19,852

John Robertson 214

The 'Heart of Midlothian' is a mosaic pattern in Edinburgh city centre, where the entrance to the Old Tolbooth jail used to be. It is also the title of a novel by Sir Walter Scott.

Hibernian

(Hibs, The Hibees)

1875

Easter Road

20,421

Gordon Smith 303

Edinburgh side Hibs were the first British side to play in the European Cup. They reached the semi-final of the very first competition in the 1955/56 season.

Inverness Caledonian Thistle
(Caley Thistle)

1994 — Caledonian Stadium — 7,512 — Billy McKay 103

Caley Thistle were formed from the merger of two clubs, Caledonian and Inverness Thistle. They rose from the bottom division to the top in just 10 years.

Kelty Hearts
(The Maroon Machine)

1975   New Central Park   2,181   Stuart Cargill 167

Kelty Hearts were promoted from the Lowland League in 2021, and again to League One the following year. They share a name and colours with Heart of Midlothian.

Kilmarnock

(Killie)

1869   Rugby Park   15,003   Bill Culley 82

Kilmarnock are one of only a few Scottish clubs to have played in three European competitions – the European Cup, Cup Winners' Cup and UEFA Cup.

Livingston

(Livi)

1943   Almondvale Stadium   8,716   Iain Russell 55

Formed in Edinburgh as Ferranti Thistle, the club became Meadowbank Thistle in 1974. They were renamed again in 1995 when they moved to Livingston.

Montrose

(The Gable Endies)

1879   Links Park   4,936   Bobby Livingstone 165

Montrose were the first league club to contest the pyramid play-off, in 2015. They beat Highland champions Brora Rangers to stay in League Two.

Motherwell

(The Steelmen)

1886　　Fir Park　　13,677　　Hughie Ferguson 284

Motherwell fans are said to have created the 'Viking Thunder Clap', a chant that was later made popular by supporters of the Iceland national football team in 2016.

Partick Thistle

(The Jags)

1876   Firhill Stadium   10,102   Willie Sharp 229

Partick Thistle have one of the most unusual and eye-catching mascots in world football. 'Kingsley' is an angry-looking sun, designed by famous artist David Shrigley.

Peterhead
(The Blue Toon)

1891　　　Balmoor　　　3,150　　　Rory McAllister 210

Peterhead's nickname comes from the blue woollen stockings that local fishermen used to wear. The club joined the Scottish Football League in 2000.

Queen of the South
(The Doonhamers)

 1919

 Palmerston Park

 8,690

 Jim Patterson 252

In 1956, QOS played in the first-ever Scottish match under floodlights, away to Rangers. The Dumfries club's own floodlights are the tallest in Scotland, at 26 metres high.

Queen's Park

(The Spiders)

1867   The city Stadium at Lesser Hampden   980   James McAlpine 163

Queen's Park are the only Scottish club to have played in the English FA Cup final. They did this twice, in 1884 and 1885, losing both times to Blackburn Rovers.

Raith Rovers

(The Rovers)

1883   Stark's Park   8,867   Gordon Dalziel 154

In 1994, the Kirkcaldy-based team played Bayern Munich in the UEFA Cup. They were winning 1–0 at half-time in the away tie, but lost 4–1 on aggregate.

Rangers

(The Gers)

1872   Ibrox Stadium   50,817   Jimmy Smith 381

Rangers are the only team to have won every Scottish domestic trophy. Between 2013 and 2016 they won the league titles of all three lower divisions.

Ross County

(The Staggies)

1929   Victoria Park   6,541   Gordon Connelly 101

In 1964, striker Tommy Ross broke the world record for the fastest hat-trick. He scored three goals in 90 seconds for Ross County against Nairn County.

St Johnstone
(The Saints)

1884 — McDiarmid Park — 10,696 — John Brogan 140

The Perth side won both the League Cup and Scottish Cup in 2020/21. They became only the fourth club in Scotland to do so in the same season.

St Mirren
(The Buddies)

1877   St Mirren Park   7,937   David McCrae 221

In 1890, the club from Paisley played one of the first-ever games after dark. Their game away to Morton was 'floodlit' by oil lamps.

The Spartans
(Spartans)

1951   Ainslie Park   3,612   Blair Henderson 64

The Spartans were formed in 1951 by two former Edinburgh University players. The club was originally only for graduates of the university.

Stenhousemuir

(The Warriors)

1884 Ochilview 3,746 Mark McGuigan 58

Stenhousemuir have supporters' clubs in Norway and Denmark. After 140 years of existence, they won their first league title (League Two) in 2024.

Stirling Albion
(The Binos)

 1945

 Forthbank Stadium

 3,808

 Billy Steele 129

Stirling Albion became the first British football club to play in Japan when they toured there in 1966. They beat the Japan national side 4–2.

Stranraer

(The Blues)

1870   Stair Park   4,178   Craig Malcolm 103

Stranraer have been sponsored by Stena Line since 1996 – a world record shirt sponsorship deal. Stena Line run ferries from nearby Cairnryan to Belfast.

Other Scottish clubs

Albion Rovers

Relegated to the Lowland League in 2023, the Wee Rovers play in Coatbridge. Their current floodlights were rehoused from Cardiff Arms Park.

Berwick Rangers

The team from Berwick-upon-Tweed were the only English club to play in the Scottish league until their relegation in 2019. They now play in the Lowland League.

Bonnyrigg Rose

James Bond actor Sean Connery spent two seasons playing for the Rose in the 1950s, before starting his acting career. The club played in League Two from 2022 to 2025.

Brechin City

The Hedgemen's record attendance of 8,122 (a cup game vs Aberdeen in 1973) was more than the population of the town itself. The club were relegated to the Highland League in 2021.

Clydebank

In 1993, years before Ipswich were sponsored by Ed Sheeran, the Bankies had the name of pop group 'Wet Wet Wet' on their shirts. Bought out in 2002, there is now a new club of this name.

Cowdenbeath

A Lowland League team since 2022, Cowdenbeath are nicknamed 'The Blue Brazil'. Their Central Park stadium has a wide track around the pitch, which is used for stock car racing.

East Stirlingshire

The Shire finished bottom of the Scottish Football League for 5 years in a row between 2003 and 2007. Playing in the Lowland League since 2016, they share a stadium with Falkirk.

Gretna

Gretna joined the Scottish League in 2002 and were promoted to the top division within 5 years. They got to the Scottish Cup final in 2006 but went bust in 2008.

Facts & Stats

Are you stoked about stats?

Get the lowdown on which clubs have won the most league titles and cups, which players have scored the most goals, and more!

Some pages feature further fantastic facts for the first-rate footy fanatic!

English champions

Number of league titles won

Liverpool	20
Manchester United	20
Arsenal	13
Manchester City	10
Everton	9
Aston Villa	7
Chelsea	6
Sunderland	6
Newcastle United	4
Sheffield Wednesday	4
Blackburn Rovers	3
Huddersfield Town	3
Leeds United	3
Wolverhampton Wanderers	3

Burnley	2
Derby County	2
Portsmouth	2
Preston North End	2
Tottenham Hotspur	2
Ipswich Town	1
Leicester City	1
Nottingham Forest	1
Sheffield United	1
West Bromwich Albion	1

Since the start of the Premier League (1992), Manchester United have won the title a record 13 times.

Most FA Cup wins

Arsenal	14
Manchester United	13
Chelsea	8
Liverpool	8
Tottenham Hotspur	8
Aston Villa	7
Manchester City	7
Blackburn Rovers	6
Newcastle United	6
Everton	5
Wanderers	5
West Bromwich Albion	5
Bolton Wanderers	4
Sheffield United	4
Wolverhampton Wanderers	4
Sheffield Wednesday	3
West Ham United	3
Bury	2
Nottingham Forest	2
Old Etonians	2
Portsmouth	2
Preston North End	2
Sunderland	2
Barnsley	1
Blackburn Olympic	1
Blackpool	1
Bradford City	1
Burnley	1
Cardiff City	1
Charlton Athletic	1
Clapham Rovers	1
Coventry City	1
Crystal Palace	1
Derby County	1
Huddersfield Town	1
Ipswich Town	1
Leeds United	1
Leicester City	1
Notts County	1
Old Carthusians	1
Oxford University	1
Royal Engineers	1
Southampton	1
Wigan Athletic	1
Wimbledon	1

Clubs with the same number are highlighted in the same colour

Biggest Premier League wins

Season	Home team	Result	Away team
1994/95	Manchester United	9-0	Ipswich Town
2019/20	Southampton	0-9	Leicester City
2020/21	Manchester United	9-0	Southampton
2022/23	Liverpool	9-0	Bournemouth
1999/20	Newcastle United	8-0	Sheffield Wednesday
2009/10	Tottenham Hotspur	9-1	Wigan Athletic
2009/10	Chelsea	8-0	Wigan Athletic
2012/13	Chelsea	8-0	Aston Villa
2014/15	Southampton	8-0	Sunderland
2019/20	Manchester City	8-0	Watford
2023/24	Sheffield United	0-8	Newcastle United

The highest-scoring Premier League match was Portsmouth's 7-4 win at home to Reading on 29 September 2007.

Fastest Premier League goals

Season	Player	Home team	Away team	Time (sec)
2018/19	Shane Long	Watford	Southampton	7.69
2022/23	Philip Billing	Arsenal	Bournemouth	9.11
2000/01	Ledley King	Bradford City	Tottenham	9.82
2024/25	Abdoulaye Doucouré	Everton	Leicester City	10.18
2002/03	Alan Shearer	Newcastle	Man City	10.52
2017/18	Christian Eriksen	Tottenham	Man Utd	10.54
2000/01	Mark Viduka	Charlton	Leeds	11.90
1995/96	Dwight Yorke	Coventry	Aston Villa	12.16
1994/95	Chris Sutton	Everton	Blackburn	12.94
2003/04	Kevin Nolan	Blackburn	Bolton	13.48
2004/05	James Beattie	Chelsea	Southampton	13.52
2013/14	Asmir Begović	Stoke	Southampton	13.64
2013/14	Jay Rodriguez	Chelsea	Southampton	13.68
2013/14	Jesús Navas	Man City	Tottenham	13.76
2018/19	Naby Keïta	Liverpool	Huddersfield	15.20

The team that scored the goal is highlighted darker

Top scorers in the Premier League

Player	Goals	Goals for each club
Alan Shearer	260	Newcastle Utd 148, Blackburn Rovers 112
Harry Kane	213	Tottenham Hotspur 213
Wayne Rooney	208	Manchester Utd 183, Everton 25
Andy Cole	187	Man Utd 93, Newcastle Utd 43, Blackburn Rovers 27, Fulham 12, Man City 9, Portsmouth 3
Mohamed Salah	186	Liverpool 184, Chelsea 2
Sergio Agüero	184	Manchester City 184
Frank Lampard	177	Chelsea 147, West Ham Utd 24, Man City 6
Thierry Henry	175	Arsenal 175
Robbie Fowler	163	Liverpool 128, Man City 21, Leeds Utd 14
Jermain Defoe	162	Tottenham 91, Sunderland 34, West Ham Utd 18, Portsmouth 15, Bournemouth 4

Andy Cole, Alan Shearer and Mohamed Salah share the record for number of goal involvements (goals + assists) in a single season – 47.

The English Premier League has been going since 1992

Top scorers in the Scottish Premiership

Player	Goals	Goals for each club
Leigh Griffiths	92	Celtic 90, Dundee 2
James Tavernier	84	Rangers 84
Alfredo Morelos	78	Rangers 78
Adam Rooney	66	Aberdeen 66
Odsonne Édouard	66	Celtic 66
Lawrence Shankland	64	Dundee Utd 8, Hearts 56
Kyōgo Furuhashi	63	Celtic 63
Liam Boyce	62	Ross County 48, Hearts 14
Billy Mckay	59	Inverness CT 32, Ross County 15, Dundee Utd 12
James Forrest	59	Celtic 59

In March 2024, James Tavernier became British football's highest-scoring defender ever, with 131 goals in all competitions.

The Scottish Premiership has been going since 2013

Scottish champions

Number of league titles won

Celtic	55
Rangers	55
Aberdeen	4
Heart of Midlothian	4
Hibernian	4
Dumbarton	2
Dundee	1
Dundee United	1
Kilmarnock	1
Motherwell	1
Third Lanark	1

The very first Scottish league title, in season 1890/91, was shared between Rangers and Dumbarton.

Most Scottish Cup wins

Celtic	42
Rangers	34
Queen's Park	10
Aberdeen	8
Heart of Midlothian	8
Clyde	3
Hibernian	3
Kilmarnock	3
St Mirren	3
Vale of Leven	3
Dundee United	2
Dunfermline Athletic	2
Falkirk	2
Motherwell	2
Renton	2
St Johnstone	2
Third Lanark	2

Airdrieonians	1
Dumbarton	1
Dundee	1
East Fife	1
Greenock Morton	1
Inverness Caley Thistle	1
Partick Thistle	1
St Bernard's	1

Queen's Park won the first Scottish Cup, in 1874. They went on to win another 7 of the next 12, before record holders Celtic had even been formed.

Biggest stadiums

Stadium	Capacity	Home team
Old Trafford	74,879	Manchester United
London Stadium	62,500	West Ham United
Tottenham Hotspur Stadium	62,850	Tottenham Hotspur
Anfield	61,276	Liverpool
Emirates Stadium	60,704	Arsenal
Celtic Park	60,411	Celtic
Etihad Stadium	55,097	Manchester City
Hill Dickinson Stadium	52,888	Everton
St James' Park	52,405	Newcastle United
Ibrox Stadium	50,817	Rangers

Wembley Stadium, home of the England national team, has a capacity of 90,000.

Hampden Park, home of the Scotland national team, has a capacity of 51,866.

Biggest crowds

Home domestic matches, by club.
*Some were not at their usual home ground.

Date	Match	Stadium	Crowd
2/1/1939	Rangers v Celtic	Ibrox Park	118,567
18/1/1930	Queen's Park v Rangers	Hampden Park	95,722
3/3/1934	Man City v Stoke City	Maine Road	84,569
1/1/1938	Celtic v Rangers	Celtic Park	83,500
10/2/2018	Tottenham v Arsenal	Wembley Stadium*	83,222
12/10/1935	Chelsea v Arsenal	Stamford Bridge	82,905
17/1/1948	Man United v Arsenal	Maine Road*	81,962
18/9/1948	Everton v Liverpool	Goodison Park	78,299
2/3/1946	Aston Villa v Derby County	Villa Park	76,588
8/3/1933	Sunderland v Derby County	Roker Park	75,118

The biggest crowd for a domestic match was 147,365 at Hampden Park for the 1937 Scottish Cup final between Celtic and Aberdeen.

Oldest clubs

(still playing in the league)
Year formed

England

Notts County	1862
Stoke City	1863
Wrexham	1864
Nottingham Forest	1865
Sheffield Wednesday	1867
Reading	1871
Aston Villa	1874
Bolton Wanderers	1874
Birmingham City	1875
Blackburn Rovers	1875

Scotland

Queen's Park	1867
Kilmarnock	1869
Stranraer	1870
Dumbarton	1872
Rangers	1872
Greenock Morton	1874
Hamilton Academical	1874
Heart of Midlothian	1874
Hibernian	1875
Partick Thistle	1876

The oldest recorded club was the Edinburgh-based 'Foot-Ball Club'. They played between 1824 and 1941.

Formed in 1857, Sheffield FC is the oldest existing club in the world. They play in the Northern Counties East League Premier Division, the 9th tier of English football.

Most European trophies

Club	Trophies	Details
Liverpool	14	6 CL, 3 EL, 4 SC, 1 FIFA
Chelsea	10	2 CL, 2 EL, 1 Conf, 2 CWC, 2 SC, 1 FIFA
Manchester United	8	3 CL, 1 EL, 1 CWC, 1 SC, 1 FIFA, 1 IC
Manchester City	4	1 CL, 1 CWC, 1 SC, 1 FIFA
Tottenham Hotspur	4	3 EL, 1 CWC
Nottingham Forest	3	2 CL, 1 SC
Aston Villa	3	1 CL, 1 IT, 1 SC
West Ham United	3	1 Conf, 1 CWC, 1 IT
Aberdeen	2	1 CWC, 1 SC
Arsenal	2	1 CWC, 1 FC
Leeds United	2	2 FC
Newcastle United	2	1 IT, 1 FC

CL = European Cup / Champions League
EL = UEFA Cup / Europa League
Conf = Conference League
CWC = Cup Winners' Cup
IT = Intertoto Cup
SC = Super Cup
FC = Inter-Cities Fairs Cup
FIFA = FIFA Club World Cup
IC = Intercontinental Cup

Quizzes

Are you a quiz whizz?

Test your knowledge in these
brain-bending football quizzes.
If you are stuck and need some help, look
back over the previous pages for a hint –
all of the answers can be found in this book.

Once you've finished a quiz, you can check
if your answers are correct on page 192.

Fab facts – England

1. In 1971, Blackpool beat which team in the final of the Anglo-Italian Cup?

   a. Atalanta
   b. Bologna
   c. Napoli

2. Which club has a badge featuring a submarine?

   a. Portsmouth   b. Port Vale   c. Barrow

3. Whose mascot is H'Angus the Monkey?

   a. Halifax Town   b. Harrogate Town
   c. Hartlepool United

4. Which England goalkeeper used to play for Shrewsbury?

   a. Joe Hart
   b. Jordan Pickford
   c. Nick Pope

5. How many home grounds have QPR had?

   a. Less than 10   b. 12   c. More than 12

6 Who are the only English league team to play in dark green?

a. Bromley
b. Stevenage
c. Plymouth Argyle

7 When were MK Dons formed?

a. 1889   b. 2002   c. 2004

8 Which club is the only non-English team to have won the FA Cup?

a. Cardiff City
b. Swansea City
c. Newport County

9 Crystal Palace won which trophy in 2025?

a. League Cup   b. FA Cup
c. Europa League

10 Which is the oldest professional football club in the world?

a. Nottingham Forest
b. Notts County
c. Stoke City

Fab facts – Scotland

1. **Who originally made up the Hamilton Accies team?**
   a. Postal workers
   b. School pupils
   c. University students

2. **Which Scottish club has played in England?**
   a. Annan Athletic   b. Berwick Rangers
   c. Queen of the South

3. **Which English club has played in Scotland?**
   a. Annan Athletic   b. Berwick Rangers
   c. Queen of the South

4. **Motherwell fans are said to have created what?**
   a. The vuvuzela noise
   b. The 'Mexican wave'
   c. The 'Viking Thunder Clap'

5. **When did Celtic win the European Cup?**
   a. 1887   b. 1967   c. 1976

6 When did Gretna go bust?
   a. 2002   b. 2006   c. 2008

7 Which club has the tallest floodlights in Scotland?
   a. Queen of the South   b. Queen's Park
   c. Queens Park Rangers

8 What does Partick Thistle's mascot look like?

   a. A mad moon
   b. An angry-looking sun
   c. An annoyed asteroid

9 Which Scottish club have played in the English FA Cup final?
   a. Queen of the South   b. Queen's Park
   c. Inverness Caledonian Thistle

10 Which team had the biggest-ever victory in senior football?

   a. Dundee Harp, 35-0 v Aberdeen Rovers
   b. Arbroath, 36-0 v Bon Accord
   c. Aberdeen, 37-0 v Third Lanark

Nifty nicknames

1. What is the nickname given to Newcastle United?

a. The Magpies
b. The Seagulls
c. The Canaries

2. Which club is called 'The Blades'?

a. Sheffield Wednesday
b. Sheffield United   c. Shrewsbury Town

3. Who have the nickname 'The Robins'?

a. Cheltenham Town   b. Bristol City
c. Both a and b

4. Which Scottish team are called 'The Red Lichties'?

a. Arbroath
b. Heart of Midlothian
c. Stenhousemuir

5. Which nickname is common to Barnsley and Liverpool?

a. The Blues   b. The Reds   c. The U's

6. How many teams are called 'The Dons'?
   a. One   b. Two   c. Three

7. Which team are known as 'The Stags'?
   a. Livingston
   b. Mansfield Town
   c. Newport County

8. Peterhead get their nickname from which item of clothing that used to be worn by local fishermen?
   a. Shirts   b. Shorts   c. Stockings

9. What is Sunderland's nickname?
   a. The Red Devils   b. The Black Cats
   c. The Bluebirds

10. Which club is known as 'The Posh'?
    a. Peterborough United
    b. Portsmouth
    c. Peterhead

Super stadiums

1 What is the name of Arsenal's stadium?

a. Emirates Stadium
b. Etihad Stadium
c. Highbury

2 Which team play at St Mary's Stadium?

a. Birmingham City   b. Exeter City
c. Southampton

3 What is the capacity of Anfield?

a. 62,716   b. 61,276   c. 67,216

4 Which stadium is home to Cardiff City?

a. Cardiff City Stadium
b. Ninian Park
c. Principality Stadium

5 Which club plays at the MKM Stadium?

a. Elgin City   b. Hull City   c. Lincoln City

6. The stadiums of which two teams are only 200 yards (183 metres) apart?
   a. Celtic and Rangers
   b. Dundee and Dundee United
   c. Hearts and Hibs

7. Where do Aston Villa play?
   a. Aston Park
   b. Birmingham Stadium
   c. Villa Park

8. How many fans can fit in The Valley?
   a. 17,111   b. 27,111   c. 72,111

9. Which 1937 game had the biggest-ever crowd in a domestic match?
   a. Rangers v Celtic   b. Celtic v Rangers
   c. Celtic v Aberdeen

10. The stadium of which league club has the lowest capacity (only 700)?
    a. East Fife
    b. East Kilbride
    c. West Bromwich Albion

Great goalscorers

1. Who is Manchester City's top goalscorer?
   a. Erling Haaland
   b. Sergio Agüero
   c. Wayne Rooney

2. Which club did Luther Blisset score 186 goals for?
   a. Watford   b. Wigan   c. Wrexham

3. How many goals did Joe Harper score for Aberdeen?
   a. 99   b. 199   c. 299

4. Who is the all-time top scorer in the Scottish Premiership?
   a. Ally McCoist
   b. Lawrence Shankland
   c. Leigh Griffiths

5. Harry Kane scored how many goals in total for Tottenham Hotspur?
   a. 213   b. 280   c. 283

6) In how many seconds was the fastest Premier League goal scored?

a. 7.69   b. 7.96   c. 9.67

7) Which Burnley player was the first to score a hat-trick in the English league?

a. George Beel
b. Jay Rodriguez
c. William Tait

8) Jimmy Kébé scored the fastest-ever FA Cup goal for which team?

a. Raith Rovers   b. Reading
c. Rotherham United

9) How many goals did Thierry Henry score in the Premier League?

a. 157   b. 175   c. 177

10) Who is the all-time top scorer for Stoke City?

a. Jack Connor
b. Bobby Gurney
c. John Ritchie

Name that kit!

Random brainteasers

1. How many clubs in this book play in a kit with:
   A. stripes?
   B. halves?
   C. hoops?
   D. quarters?

2. Which club have twice won the European Cup Winners' Cup?

3. In the Premier League, which team have twice lost 9-0 and once won 8-0?

4. There are two clubs nicknamed the Bees. Which two kits do they play in, a or b?

5. Who have won the most league titles, Heart of Midlothian or Huddersfield Town?
   a. Hearts   b. Huddersfield
   c. Both have won the same number

6. Who is the top scorer for two different Scottish clubs?

7. How many clubs in this book have any shade of green as their main colour?

8. Which two of these teams have never won the FA Cup?

   a. Barnsley   b. Blackpool
   c. Bolton Wanderers   d. Brentford
   e. Brighton & Hove Albion   f. Bury

9. A. How many English clubs play in a plain white kit?
   B. How many Scottish clubs play in a plain dark blue kit?

10. True or false?

    A. Crawley Town and Manchester United are both nicknamed the Red Devils.

    B. Brazil played their first-ever game against Cowdenbeath.

    C. Shane Long scored a Premier League goal in under 8 seconds.

Answers

Fab facts England
1. b
2. c
3. c
4. a
5. c
6. c
7. c
8. a
9. b
10. b

Fab facts Scotland
1. b
2. a
3. b
4. c
5. b
6. c
7. a
8. b
9. b
10. b

Nifty nicknames
1. a
2. b
3. c
4. a
5. b
6. c
7. b
8. c
9. b
10. a

Super stadiums
1. a
2. c
3. b
4. a
5. b
6. b
7. c
8. b
9. c
10. b

Great goalscorers
1. b
2. a
3. b
4. c
5. b
6. a
7. c
8. b
9. b
10. c

Name that kit!
1. Wycombe Wanderers
2. Kidderminster Harriers
3. Scunthorpe United
4. Bradford City
5. Airdrieonians
6. Hibernian
7. Crystal Palace
8. Albion Rovers
9. Queen's Park
10. Rochdale
11. West Bromwich Albion
12. Blackburn Rovers

Random brainteasers
1. A) 36*   B) 3   C) 12**   D) 2
2. Chelsea
3. Southampton
4. b
5. a
6. Blair Henderson
7. 5
8. d and e
9. A) 15   B) 4
10. A) True   B) False   C) True

*not inc. Partick Thistle
**not inc. Motherwell